# CORPUS

An Anthology of Poets in Search of God

# CORPUS

## An Anthology of Poets in Search of God

Edited by

## ALFRREDO NAVARRO SALANGA

New Day Publishers
Quezon City
1989

# PREFACE

12 September 1988

Mrs. Gloria F. Rodriguez
Director/Publisher
New Day Publishers
11 Lands Street, Project 6
1100 Quezon City

Dear Gloria:

Greetings (again).

Enclosed is another manuscript for New Day's consideration. *Corpus: An Anthology of Poets in Search of God* is a collection of religious verse that avoids the mawkishness and sentimentality of most of the poetry written in this vein. The poets whose works have been selected for this collection are among the best practitioners of the craft and their being engaged in other than their usual secular subjects may come as a pleasant surprise to many.

It is a varied selection, ranging from examinations of the folk experience of religion and Christianity (Brion, Santos, Lim, Kilates, Remoto), to the mystical experience (Gamalinda and Dimapilis in whom we see intimations of St. John of the Cross) and to the historical and theological roots of Christianity in the Philippines (Abad, Bautista, Salanga). It should also be noted that none of the poems are strictly sectarian.

At any rate, I do hope this merits New Day's approval.

Yours sincerely,

ALFRREDO NAVARRO SALANGA
5 Mabuhay Street, East Avenue
Diliman, Quezon City
Tel. 921-4756

# PUBLISHER'S NOTE

About one week apart in September 1988, our friend Freddie Salanga sent two manuscripts to New Day for possible publication. Both were subsequently approved by the Board of Trustees of the Christian Literature Society of the Philippines (the real identity of New Day Publishers, which is a non-stock, non-profit publishing society) in their next meeting.

On 15 October 1988 Alfrredo Navarro Salanga died, many of his songs unsung at the early age of 40. We continue to grieve over his non-physical presence in our midst.

With the publication of this volume of poetry which he collected and edited, as well as other publications New Day and/or other Philippine publishers may publish of his works, we hope to keep alive the values and the ideals by which Freddie lived.

GFR

# TABLE OF CONTENTS

**GEMINO H. ABAD**

## AND LET NO WORDS BREAK

Where no words break
I thirst no longer for truth,
Am very still, at peace.
    Time was
the truth was future perfect;
But I no longer seek,
all my pieces I have collected

*and let no words break*

Where no words break
my thirst is quenched
by every spring,
the spring is everywhere.
    Time was
I strove for truth,
the passion grew,
but words could not appease.
Truth had no bounds

*and let no words break*

The President whose State was a Lie,
the soldier who did not fire,
people shouting, words dying . . .
    Or fruit of achiote,
snails after, things swarming . . .
Once these were truth's sundries,
its daily exhibits,
but did not make a book

*where no words break*

I thirst no longer for truth,
Am without words composed.
Our ticks have lost their itch,
The tocks of doom have grown serene.
I no longer even roam

*where no words break*

19/20 June 1986


## THE POOR WHO ARE

    Sir,
it isn't possible to tell
who are the poor.
    For first,
we must put away our words:
our words speak us,
not the poor.
The poor like God
do not make speeches;
but we by our words have built
two great towers—
History we call one, the other Law:
by one, we found our image,
and by the other, maintain it.

O, I would tell you, sir,
who are the poor.
But they slink into our words,
their lives become our fiction:
Aborigines of our world,
without word . . .
    whom One among us
once did love.

He gave them His body,
His own broken,
—They called it their bread;
He gave them His blood,
His own spilled,
—They called it their drink.
    Speechless they
before the terror of such love.

He became their only word.

But still their hovels
gut our space;
our towering words
their silence devour.
    Behold,
the poor who are:
outside our words
by which history and law
are made.
    Sir,
they have no language yet.


[Author's note: "Originally, the poem was called 'Like FLies'; I have
since revised it.  G.H.A. 30 December 1984]

# ARCHANGEL OF GETHSEMANE

(A Christmas Parable)

The poor families around the plush village of Gethsemane were especially devoted to Gabriel the Archangel, believing that one day he would himself announce the Good News to them and, riding a star like their Christmas *parol*, lead them out of captivity—as with the Three Kings of old—toward God's own Son, Firstborn of the poor. Fr. Cruz encouraged their faith for it gave them the pure comfort of a delusion.

Throughout the year, the poor kept to their shanties. But at Christmas, their children would go about in random carolling with empty cans and sticks, and on the great day itself of our Savior's birth, lead their elders in scattered droves over Gethsemane. In full force, husbands, wives, children poured out into the streets and knocked at the high gates, the children piping "Merry Christmas! Merry Christmas!" as they were taught in school. Their din and insistent music of the doorbell would bring the housemaids down to them, with candies and leftovers, but the times being hard, they preferred even small change for it was money to hand. Often they went away sad, but hopeful again at the next gate whose huge, intricate parol promised a share in the hidden wealth.

This practice provided for years the only link between rich and poor in Gethsemane. But one day, Mr. de Jesus spoke up at the village council: "Let us be honest for once. We give out of fear only, or perhaps, just to be rid of the annoyance. The poor sense this, and press their advantage, for they are sly and laugh at us." Mr. Reyes shook his head: "Fear? What harm can the poor do us? They obey our laws and have no arms." Then Don Emmanuel Pascua observed with a smile: "Despite our laws, we leave these squatters alone. They should return the favor." And so they issued a decree that henceforth the poor should apply at the parish office or a nearby branch of the Ministry of Social Services. Thereby, the legal residents could rest and have a tranquil time for themselves during Christmas.

And so it came to pass that, in the year of Our Lord 1984, Gethsemane slept in peace for the first time. At the first *Misa de Gallo*, Fr. Cruz praised the village council for its efficiency. The Great Day of Christmas came and passed without trouble. The streets were deserted and housemaids felt relieved. A few poor families who thought little of decrees were directed to the parish office for hot soup. Only the children of the rich were oppressed by the day's silence. Knowing nothing of councils or decrees, they became listless at play amidst their gifts from Santa.

As the Great Day ended, a strange event took place that, for fear of ridicule, the press itself censored. Yet it could not be kept secret by housemaids, and soon everyone talked about it, although no explanation could be found.

It seems that soon after dark, the poor families strode out in procession—husbands, wives, children, all in their best Sunday clothes, and singing in incredibly sweet voices. A wondrous sight! Their faces shone with an unearthly glow, not alone from the lighted parol that each one bore. And leading the procession was a resplendent figure, his wings about him like a great cloak. His face shone like lightning and his garments were as white as snow. The rich looked over their gates with fear, but their children ran out joyously into the streets. In a moment, the procession vanished in a coruscating wake of stars, and a deathly stillness fell upon Gethsemane.

A wild panic then gripped every family. "The children! Where have our children gone?" A great cry of anguish rose up to heaven. But the procession had gone like a dream. Swiftly, villagers and police raided the shanties. The poor had simply left all their belongings behind, food on the table, working tools, small change. Not a single soul was to be found. Only dogs wandered about, moaning for their lost masters whose smell still lingered in the muddy footpaths and deserted backyards.

(Written 30 December 1984)

# WAITING

Wrapped in finery,
I have waited for this.
My hands are folded
Like plaster wings.
I have stretched my stare
Across the firmament
Where the air has built
Its nest. From the shadows,
Bats and prayers brush
Against the heavy pane,
Rushing to be freed.
My lips are sealed in place.
I have longed to fill
Abysmal niches with the fire
And incense from my candle
And softly tread as in
Procession down the empty aisle.
My tabernacle would
Its door wrench open
If only for the saints, who
Stupefied, intercede
Not for me, look down on me.
I had waited until the pews
Tired under my weight.

## MARKETPLACE

Here
In the marketplace
Above the haggling
And the cackling
We have arrived

Here
Where the air ferments
The darkness settling
On the putrid flesh

Inside out
Cut up
Once cleansed with water
Turned to wine

Now denied

As the cock stripped
Of its crow
The fish refusing
Replication

Here in the entombment
Of wooden stalls
And staves

Now and at the hour

We wring the prayer
Of twilight.

**ROFEL G. BRION**

## TO THE ONE I LOOK UP TO

For years you have pierced me
With your brooding eyes
Threatened by deep red drops
From a forehead wrapped in thorns.

What do you want from me?

Do you want me to pull out
The nails that kiss your palms and feet,
To wipe off with my lips
The jewel of blood on your chest?

What do you want me to do?

Do you want me to undress
And stretch out on your cross
So you can gaze at me
Without nails, without wounds,
With no crown of thorns?

## PANE SCULPTORS

—who that thug is,
entombed beyond the glass.
We stare,
robbed.
It is milky,
this glass, and resists
our eyes' penetration
however much we rub.

And so we are seduced:
the endless labor

—that ends only in death:
—stretched out on the floor
emaciated, in rags,
amid stone, clutching
hammer and chisel,

the glass finally blank

## HAIKU & VARIATION OF A MANTRA

To be the vision
itself, pulse and prelude
of an angel shattered.

Gone, gone from me, gone
from me forever, a rain
of brilliant fevers.

## TOMASINO SEARCHES FOR THE DALAI LAMA

*. . . and where does the river end?*
At the world's edge, its shifting
of carrion and coral.

*And what instructs our departures?*
Follow the pulsar before you.
Speak its language, here at death's dusty junction.

*What shall we see along the way?*
Wings and things; bones and thrones;
its aftermath of silt and silk.

*What will he be like?*
The minor of your hopes. Yet his small hands
will extinguish you.

*At what cost?*
The shimmer of found speech,
or hymn's sudden lucency.


## INDULANIN 14


"Ach, wen vermogen wir denn zu brauchen?
Engel nicht, Menschen nicht . . ."

What shall he say if I move my shadow
to his greater shade? I should be silenced
by his inner midnight, ordinary
in his oceans of shimmering lyric.
And my voice, reaching him, should hardly stir him

out of the lengths and distances of sleep;
and our petty histories should mean nothing to him,
who plots grander schemes and cannot be concerned
with the cliff-edge where we teeter, two by two.
The view's magnificent from here, where God

seems no more nor less than the ordinary man;
and yet his vaster sorrow spreads its wings

and break now color on our lives and things:
it is always in us, murmuring Ich kann, Ich kann.

1984

## LA NAVAL DE MANILA:
## SELIM SOT AS A MODERN POLITICAL OBSERVER

Things turn mortal at twilight.
Six years at sea, and I am attuned
to the skulls of mystery: that dark
should spare no one, arrabal

of moonlight is love's betrayal;
we thrive on things ephemeral.
I say I am unmmoved by it.
I have met the opportune fevers

where they dawdle or malinger.
Staggering into the *avenidas
de las felicidades* I burn
where it matters: I claim dominion

over oracles, wounds. All this mourning
distends the senses, plucks from star
or sprint of cloud some vast
insouciant theophany, wanton

hope in the providence of gods, et
cetera. I have seen night's dogs
howl and scratch the tombstones
for my name. I have watched the hands

move where they may, contraband
but beautiful in the dusklight
with hint of down and Faure hissing,
melancholy on the tape. I have said

the proper words, bled just so, disbursed
such promises as vow eternity; in short
I've made my peace. And the little that I vow
I disenthrall so often. My words, sure and fluid

as meteors, assume the orbits
of beatitudes, bright testaments.
What am I then, sputtering syllabi
of supernovas? Another dragon?

I scuttle to the naked christ
who skims among the muscled seraphim
and is moved by instinct to extinguish me.
Now all the world stoops to accept

his benediction, while forgotten armies
sludge across the sleepy cenacles
where admirals exhume their favored
speech, figments of their x y z's.

———————

When the armada of the Cross under John of Austria, brother of
Philip II, defeated the naval armies of the Crescent under Selim the
Sot off the gulf of Lepanto in the Ionian Sea, the victory of the Chris-
tians was attributed to the Queen of the Most Holy Rosary, thereafter
known as La Naval de Lepanto. The year was 1571. The day was the
first Sunday of October. Seventy-five years later similar naval victories
in the Philippine archipelago would be attributed to La Naval de
Manila.

## KAGSAWA

The past preserves its durable ruin.
Keeping all, it denies its own oblivion.
Behold the goat-path, bramble, cogon
Over cobblestone, mortar crumbling.
Brown hands shaped this roofless wall
Now leaning; alien vision instructed
Their worship and submission, held
Their awe and selfhood in thrall.
Both are clutched by vine and root:
When sky dimmed and the Volcano's mouth
Glowed, the priest shuddered at the Elevation;
When stones rained and the earth shook,
Death brought its vague and fearful liberation,
The past preserved its durable ruin.


From Marne Kilates. *Children of the Snarl and Other Poems*


## THE SEXTON AT HIS DOTAGE

White ants eat at the wood
Of the stair to the bells,
The steps complain at each step,
And tremble every Vespers.
The children mock me
And are no longer afraid
Of the headless friar I conjure
With each warning against

Their endless journeys to the belfry.
Bats nest at the gap where the stone
Supports the *kamagong* crossbeams
Bearing the bronze giant cast in Toledo,
They linger longer and return too soon
After the dying of each vibration.
The stone steps to this church on a hill,
Held together by ancient mortar-and-honey,
Seem steeper each day, are loose
Like teeth, and I lose count
And confuse the order of *Plata, Mata, Oro.*
The old limbs have gone stiff,
The wind from the acacias hurts my joints,
It takes too much to ring the fiesta *repique.*
The wire cables and wood levers
Swinging the clappers have become
Stubborn and heavy. Daylight seems
Too soon for the priests' Matins,
And they have taken somebody else
As Sacristan Mayor to attend
To the baptisms and weddings,
The lighting of the Paschal Candle,
The rousing of the people at Easter Sunday.
And they call me only for the requiems
At dusk, to accompany the chanting
Of the *Liberame Domine.*


# THE PASSION OF DONALD REXFORD, JR.


*Donald Rexford, Jr., Filipino 'G.I. baby' born out of the Second World War, has vowed to re-enact the Crucifixion, literally, every Good Friday, until he finds his American father.*

Upon this flat Golgotha
Of an abandoned ricefield,
Where the sparse grass redeems the soil
Only to sprout a slum or a subdivision,
My cruelest month again descends.

At three o'clock of the Friday afternoon
Of the Sacred Week, the nails will pierce
My oft-pierced hands and feet,
My cross will rise for five minutes,
My yearly vow will be fulfilled.

World, let my father know,
By TV network and news syndicate,
That I am here.

Father, redeem this laundrywoman's son
You sired at the close of the last War,
Conceived unimmaculate in the smoke
Of D-Day and the lust of Marine sergeants,
And forsaken in the oblivion of post-Liberation.

Confirm my name, my identity
That by *jus sanguinis* belongs
To the Greatest Nation on Earth,
The modern Romans who ravished my country
But who are also my people.

Transport me, by this rite of the Greatest Sufferer,
From this despoiled Gethsemane
Of starvation wages and unemployment,
To the New Paradise
Of social welfare and hamburgers.

Into thy hands I commend my citizenship.

# QUIAPO

**The Procession of the Black Nazarene**

On the ninth day of January,
In the sober days that follow the intoxicated season,
The prophets descend like tongues of fire
Upon the streets of Quiapo.
The sun bleeds its flesh of asphalt,
Scorches its bones of concrete.
Fumes issue from its pores in a heady breath,
And the air is thick.

Men, their headbands filled with sweat,
Their eyes wild with lightning,
Bare their backs tumid with pain and illusion,
Amoks for a day's season. In a frenzy,
They struggle to keep on their shoulders
Some splinter of Calvary, some chafe of the rope
That will deepen the wounds of the flesh, draw blood
To cleanse the wounds of the spirit.
In their drunken vigor, madness expiates.

God, clad in maroon, lace, gold-leaf and brocade
(Men's lame imitations of the eternal),
His eyes wild with lightning,
Stumbles forward in all directions.
But in the demented martyrdom of mortals,
Aching shoulders and bleeding flesh
Bear Him an eternity aloft.

And the prophets descend like tongues of fire
(The planets tilt in their ancient dance)
Upon the streets of Quiapo,
Upon the heedless multitude of the orange fire,
The sacred soot that asphyxiates the soul,
The spears of sun that transfix the flesh.

Our Father,
In the drug of incense,
In the burning fever of flowers,
In the heady camphor of our endless ardor,
In our faith in the Apocalypse,
In the grime on the ginseng root,
The soot on the novena,
In the wax on the bronze amulet,
The soiled sampaguita—

Heal
All these wounds You inflict on us:
On our shoulders that bear
The weight of Rulers and Nations,
On our breasts that ache and hurt with rage,
On our knees scraped in ignorance and submission,
On our ankles numb in the clamp of shackles,
On our palms pierced by nails of myriad metal,
Dipped in perfume and arsenic,
Bile and vinegar,
Mud and myrrh.


## THE BEGGARS OF MAUNDY THURSDAY


In the white light of the Lenten afternoon,
The sun resurrects them from ages
Long gone—these minions of want,
This hobbling throng, clad in the browned
Habits of their infinite bedragglement.
Issuing from the cracks on the winding
Road, among slabs loosed by the roots
Of acacia, they stir the dust
And crunch the gravel, their tin cups
Shaking with the hollow rattle of change.
What troves of their scavenging

Weigh down the bags slung at the crooks
Of elbow, the hollows of shoulder?
No burden of season nor oblivion
Can bend or muddy them still, but
Their straw hats, hoods or shawls conceal
The stares alert for dole or discard,
In the long noons of their perambulation.

They gather at the convent door
Of the stone church on the hill, lining
The walls, clustering close in their
Slow stooping movements, merging
Into the stone like moss. Three o'clock
Tolls, and ricebirds take flight
From their foraging among gaps
In the stone columns carved with saints.
The sexton opens the groaning wooden doors,
And an obese friar emerges, squinting
Into the light. From a burlap bag
Of collections he dispenses the charity
Of the faithful, delivering a solemn
Homily on the sin of sloth, the virtue
Of work, the cleansing of the spirit
In the mortification of the flesh,
The deliverance from our sins by Him
Whose suffering we now commemorate, and how
In the end the meek shall inherit the earth.

Scrutinizing their blessings, the stooped
Figures bow over their palms. The tin cups
Rattle. The ricebirds hover in a dark
Fluttering, or alight chirping among
The slabs of pavement, picking bits
Of straw or seed among the scraggly growth
Of weed, until they are driven again
In a quickening rustle as the main bell
Summons the old wives and widows
For the Via Crucis devotions.
His holy act done, the obese friar
Returns to the musty dark of his convent.

The sexton tugs at the wire cables
To ring the last summons. As the saints
In heaven resume their chores before
The Passion. And the beggars put on
Their straw hats or hood their shawls against
The long noons of their perambu'ation.


# STO. NIÑO OF NEPA-Q


Veined arms,
The color of burnt mahogany,
Cradle you from your green pedestal,
Holding you close to the sweating chest,
Your stiff, brocaded,
Gold-braided scarlet cape
Gleaming against the soiled shirt,
O innocent-eyed
Child King of the Marketplace

> *Who will buy my Sto. Niño, Rey del Mundo,*
> *Who will buy!*

Your eyes shine
Amid cherub cheeks flushed with enamel rouge
Daubed by some unknown Boticelli,
Your fingers fold
In that gesture of blessing and empire,
Gothic and feudal,
Touching the air,
Anointing the clamor of your haggling vassalage.

Look upon these
Your unmindful faithful poking through the pork,
Gill of fish,
Claw of crab,

Slab of beef,
Under lean leaves,
Among fat fruit, whorl of cabbage,
Peeling skin of onion and garlic,
Harvest of cooking oil, vinegar and soy,
Clove and seed of condiment,
Mound of salt,
Packet of chemical flavor
That soothe and deceive
The numb and finical palate.

>    *Who will buy my Sto. Niño, Rey del Mundo,*
>    *Who will buy!*

Over the howl and whine
of grinder and scale;
Over the prattle and bicker
Of chopper and board;
Over the dull thud
That cleaves the cranium of coconut
Into the halfmoons of whiteness;
Over the groan of the grater
In the shredding of flesh
To yield milk that will thicken the soup
In the stewing of stalk and leaf
And sweeten the delicacy of root and ricecake

Over these you claim dominion,
Thrive in the fealty
Of housewife and grocer,
Fishmonger and butcher,
Locksmith, lockpicker,
Filcher, pickpocket,
Hawker, ogler, wheeler-dealer,
Jack-of-all-trades,
Vendor and consumer, seekers
Of a thousand viands and cures
For a thousand hungers and urgencies.

*Who will buy my Sto. Niño, Rey del Mundo,*
*Who will buy!*

Bless the wizened woman,
Haggard and gnarled
As the tuber of ginger she holds;
Bless the scant trove of her subsistence
Gathered into the empty belly
Of her wicker basket;
Bless the small change she will fish
From her skirt to choose
From the cheaper stack of eggs
With the shells cracked and smeared.

*Who will buy my Sto. Niño, Rey del Mundo,*
*Who will buy!*

Bless the serving maid
Weighed down by the day's purchase
As she trudges behind her fair mistress
Who shields her nose
With immaculate handkerchief
As they negotiate the puddles and the filth.

*Who will buy my Sto. Niño, Rey del Mundo,*
*Who will buy!*

Bless the gamin girl
Thrusting at you her precious lemons;
Bless the sunburnt madonna
Suckling her babe among the watermelons.

*Who will buy my Sto. Niño, Rey del Mundo,*
*Who will buy!*

Bless the famished urchin
Supplicating before the stalls of smoked fish;
Bless the tax collector updating the figures
On his frayed and crumbling list.

> *Who will buy my Sto. Niño, Rey del Mundo,*
> *Who will buy!*

Bless the frantic housewife
Searching for her purse
As policeman and pickpocket split the loot
In the stench of the public toilet.

> *Who will buy my Sto. Niño, Rey del Mundo,*
> *Who will buy!*

Bless the empty bowl of soup.

Bless these,
O Child King of the Marketplace,
With your fingers folded
In that gesture of empire,
With your glass eyes of innocent power,
Sparkling in the stare of the electric glare,
Gazing from the pale illuminations
Caught in the sweating arms of market-hands,
On the thin blood of loins and steaks,
On the droplets sprinkled on fruits and leaves,
On the moisture of polythelene packets,
The fishscales clinging to the hem of skirts,
Glistening in the drainage,
Washed by the monsoon
Under catwalk and embankment,
Into the throats of the street,
In the trade of hunger and surfeit,
In the prolonging of life,
In the assuaging of our daily need.

**FATIMA LIM**

## FROM *THE FORBIDDEN TREE*

(*for f.r., tempter*)

How lovely it must have been
The tree set distinctly apart
From the others.
The peaches, dates and nectarines
Must have paled
In their bland perfection.
Not even the singing, shimmering
Birds darting from branch
To luminous branch could distract her
As much as the sinister rustling
Of the ferruginous leaves
And the upright snake
Speaking sweetly
With its forked tongue.

Perhaps she was just bored.
Bored with the man
Of the missing rib
Who was beginning to repeat
Himself, having run out of names
For the rest of the world.
Perhaps she felt
A shared companionship
With the snake
Who had only sought
A true and absolute wisdom.
It is not too clear now.
All she can recall

Is the first bite:
How her mouth filled
With meaningless tears
and spilt blood.
Roughly, she is awakened
By the snake's crazed dancing
On its hideous feet
And by her mate's calling forth
Of her name, over and over
From a distance.
The marred fruit
Rolls away from her fingers.
She tries to shield
With her less
Than adequate hands
The tremulous expanse
Of her nakedness.


## THE MEDIUM

*(for Didi and Danton, witnesses)*


I am called
The Old Woman with the Holy Child's voice.
He comes through me at the oddest moments:
Just as I am about to skive the carrots
For my husband's broth,
Wipe the dust off the cracks
Of my father's father's face, in oil
Or in the middle of my setting out
The dish of milk
For my neighbor's nameless cat.

I am told afterwards
That I go stiff as a plank.

My eyes ricochet
And a cloud forms about my singing lips.
But I am reassured that I do no harm.
The voice speaking through me has the ring
Of rain, glass beads and closed-eyed nestlings.

I awaken, remembering nothing.
Someone is grasping my right hand
His eyes gleaming with gratitude.
Someone else backs off
As if touched by fire
Or confronted with a full-length mirror.
Their secrets have been sung
By my voice. Some will return;
The others flee.

The first time it happened,
I was sitting in silence
My stillborn child's unworn clothes—
The knitted boots, jacket and cap—
Falling from my hands.
My husband caught me in his arms,
Baffled by the child's voice
And my man's weight.
But he has since kissed me
With reverence. Not wanting
To understand, or wrench my secret
From me, my dear Joseph
Finds his comfort in dreams.

My growing powers startle me.
Sometimes, I see frogs leaping
From the mouths of great men.
The lighted shells
Of still-distant years.
And the contents of coffins.
When I touch the open sores,
They seal, like midnight flowers
Before my eyes.

But I am not frightened.
There are even moments
When I am left to myself,
To burrow in the core of silence.
I sit, my fingers on my lap,
The cat in a frieze by my feet
While the Child
Leaps exultant, in the tabernacle
Of my womb.


## THE ROSARY HOUR


The women in my family
Bow their heads reverently
Over their beads.
It is the crepuscular hour.
The sun
Through the altar room
Curtains
Burns roses.

It is a Friday
In October.
I swim
Through a vale of tears.
Pilate's
Heavy rings
Clink against
The washbowl.
Veronica gasps,
Unfolding the roughened
Cloth.
And Mary Magdalene
Feeling the tremor
In her breast,

Steels herself
Against
The earth's toss
And the darkest hour.

Night comes.
We unhinge our knees.
I rush
Into the streets
Daring the onrush
Of traffic.
I am, after all,
Guarded by a legion
Of cherubims—
Those blessed creatures
Heavy-headed
With moth-like wings.

The stars glint.
They are the tears
Of gratitude
Of the pagan babes
And of my dear,
But decadent relatives
Beatific
And propelled
By my prayers
Out of their
Cage of flames.

When I step
On the crawling night
Creatures,
I do it deliberately
Just as she would
Have crushed
The head
Of the veneniferous
Snake.

And when I stand
On the rim
Of the open
Manhole,
I do it gracefully,
Just as she would
Have balanced
Herself
On the razor's edge
Of the sickle
Moon.

## MARIA

Blue grains of light
from the open window.
Whirring of wind
in the dark.

Whispers the angel
into my ear:
"Mother you will be
Of God's own Son."

"How could that be
when I am clean
as light?"
But my knees melt

In silence.
Grains of light
begin seeding
              the dark.

## HYMN

Lord who will never die:
Build a nest in the vines
of our veins. Crush
the black worm crawling
in the leaves of our hearts.
Hang a hammock for our minds.

Shadow and Light
in the loneliness of life,
East and West
of our many journeys,
we will drop anchor
in the skin of your harbor.


## THE TAAL CHURCH

as Seen from a Small Island
(*for Tita and Jun*)


My faith is softer
than the tongue of sand
of this small island.

On the highest hill
in the old town of Taal
you sit, still,

Gray like rain
between leaf and sky.
Even if the mouth

Of the sea reclaims
this tongue of sand
again and again

You will still sit,
gray like rain
            between leaf and sky.

## A DRUG ADDICT'S STO. NIÑO

He must have started and finished
the six-inch icon
at the start and finish
of a nightmarish, narcotic stimulation.

For the fruit of
regimented rehabilitation
is ridiculously misshapen,
crude as a child's
first crayon configuration
but lacking
its innocent disregard of
symmetry and instruction.

The crown has the shape of
chewed-up bubblegum
spewed out of a mouth
grown bitter
with the taste of tasteless rubber.
The space has two suspicious periods
for eyes, a nose painfully bent
to the left, and lips contorted
into a red pucker.

The hand creeping out of
a shabby, crumpled red robe
with white blotches
has no fingers. It is raw flesh
the color of half-fried spoiled fish.
The right hand bearing
the symbolic globe-world
is, once more, flesh petrifying
beneath a tiny, blue ball of plaster.

Surprisingly, the feet
are etched with five fingers each
but made to stand
on a pedestal painted to look
like a cross between melting
rocky road ice cream and a messed-up
slice of chocolate cake adorned with
lewdly green topping.

The icon is wrapped
with old newspaper
and offered to motorists with bloodshot eyes
waiting at street corners
waiting, waiting, waiting
for the red light
to turn green.

# JESUS S. M. DIMAPILIS

## PAEAN FOR MY TREMENDOUS LOVER

*(Fifteen Song-poems in Celebration of the Trilogy of Man, the Universe, and the Pervasive Love Who Sustains Life on the Planet Earth)*
        *First published in* Focus Philippines *(2 February 1985 and 23 March 1985) under the pen name Michelle Marie Rosarie*

## 1. *A SONG FOR MY FATHER*

My Father, my tremendous lover:
Pardon my daring.
Do I presume to speak to you?
Dare I address this puny voice
To one who knows my thoughts
Before they explode as words
Out of my mouth, wild flowers
Erupting from the arid sterility
Of my desert, my dry, dry heart?
Shall I now speak my errant thoughts?
Or shall I write upon the sands
What you can read so clearly
Forming in my hazy mind:
Visions and dreams of you
Walking the earth
In fervid, restless search
For me, your lost one?
Yes, though you speak to me
From the depths of your silence,
I hear your call.
You call me by name.

34

## 2. *TO THE FATHER I CANNOT SEE TODAY*

Father, my own true Father,
Father of us all,
Father of the universe
Of vast galaxies and countless stars,
Father of our enormous sun
And the great planets
And their many moons,
Forgive this little one
Daring to address you as Father.
For it is true that you have known me
Even before I was a fetus
In my mother's womb.
(But then you've known that womb
Even before it was a womb.)
You are my father indeed,
Though I have not fully known you,
Though I have not seen you.
You have called me by name,
Even before I could listen
To your eternal voice,
Long before anyone in the world
Gave me the name you willed for me.


## 3. *CHAMBERED LOVE UNLOCKED*

In truth invisible, but discernible,
Yours was the fiat
Which called forth the specific sperm
To wed the particular ovum
You anointed for me
In the secret, silent implosion
Of chambered love.
And the embryo, the fetus

Procreated in love's tight,
Passionate embrace,
Became child, became me,
Someone imaged after your heart.
For if with the single will
Of your powerful mind
You willed the stars, the suns,
To whirl and condense
Out of dust and gases
To become spheres of fire
And light in the firmament,
Then with a single act
Of your eminent will
You summoned new life
To be engendered
In intermingled blood
Of passion, and momentary death.


## 4.  *HYMN TO LOVE*


Indeed, you summoned me to life,
Long before my mother,
Whom you also fathered,
Long before my father,
Whom you also fathered,
Heard the first faint
Stirrings of my coming.
And though they heard not your voice
But only the pulsing of blood
Thundering desire in their veins,
They obeyed your sovereign will
Without really knowing,
Without sensing your presence
In the rites of wedlock
Consummated on the bed.
This, then, my Father,

Is my hymn to you, my song,
In celebration of love,
Your tremendous love
Which brought me forth
From the womb of darkness
And nothingness
Into the bosom of your light,
Into the warm glow of your love.


## 5.   THE MUSIC OF YOUR UNIVERSE


Each night I lie down
To rest, to sleep,
To die to the world
Of shapes and color,
Of sound and light,
To die in you,
Only to wake anew in you.
You wake me up.
Each day I awake
I see your face of glory
In the heavens
In the sun,
In the orange-gold fire,
The sunfire of morning
Splintered into shards of light
Upon the prism windows
Of my puny mind,
And I am born again in you
To the soundless music
Of your great universe.
This is your home, Father,
So huge I cannot see
All sides and corners of it,
So vast I cannot tell where
It begins and where it ends.

But in your great heart,
The great heart of love
You allow me to touch and feel,
I can only listen to the urgent
But gentle, gentle but restive
Throb of your love:
My Father's love.


## 6.   *THE WAY THAT LEADS TO YOU*

And though indeed sometimes
I stand at the forked road of time,
I stand still, unable to discern
Which road leads to nowhere,
Or to the cliff, to the dark edge
Where wayward spirits plunge
To perversity, or obscurity,
Lost in the seething flames
Of holocausts to idols
Of self-will and public adulation,
Human acclamation and laurels
That swell the heart of felt
And leatherette, of nylon skin
And silicon flesh, of polyester veins
Thirsty for the onrushing torrent
Of fermented blood of grapes,
The bloodied golden calf
Killed and grilled over live coals
To fatten bullapes
Bursting at the belly with gold
And silver coins and diamonds cold
With the fire of a million years.
Father: where is the one true road
That leads to you? Take me by the hand.

## 7.  *LOVER'S WAIT FOR THE BELOVED*

I know that somewhere
Beyond the sudden rise
Of road and hill
And ancient rock
You wait for my homecoming,
Restless as you pace
Back and forth,
But always anxious,
Always scanning
The horizons of my time,
Ready to run to meet me
Beyond the halfway point
To the gate,
Ready to embrace me
In your vast universal arms.

Because you love us all,
You love me no less, no more,
There's enough love for all.
In the pupil of your eye
All our picayune hearts
You can contain.


## 8. *ETERNITY CLOISTERED IN A DEWDROP*

I saw you lately in the cloistered
Mind of a nun, up on the promontory
Of a convent garden overlooking
The chapel where you dwell
In breadlike silence,
Waiting upon kneeling reverence
As you hear collective paeans
Of thanksgiving, and psalms

Of joy and pain.
For you have been enthroned
On sacrifice of lips
On praises resounding
Throughout a universe of halls
And doored rooms and crystal windows
Closed against the misty cold
Of mountain wind.
In the garden of contemplation,
I heard the chastened lips
Proclaim delight in finding you
Encased as atoms of sunlight
Captive in dewdrops
Clinging in tentative peace
To pine needles up on the trees
On the road to Bekkel.

For within the prism of a dewdrop,
Brief of tenure, tentative but
Poised serenely
In that mountain morning,
We beheld your glory,
Encapsulated in molecules
Of hydrogen and oxygen,
Your sacred spirit consenting
To captivity within a split second
Of eternity.
Before the light and heat
And warmth of your love
Evaporated dew into mist,
Rainbows cascading out
Of liquid prisms
Could only echo a fraction,
A passage from the endless
Jubilation, the staple of angels
Ministering eternal songs of joy.

## 9.  *YOUR LIKENESS IMAGED IN MEN*

For you are truly great, Father,
And no one is greater.
The sum total of all we know,
Men's vaunted synergy of knowledge,
Stored in books and microchips,
Retrieved in years and milliseconds,
Cannot compare with your
Eternal wisdom,
Wider and longer and deeper
Than the width, the length
And the depth of the vast universe,
Faster than the billion light years
Racing across the timeless void.
Yet in your deep, fathomless wisdom
You mirror your inscrutable image
In billions of petty, puny men.
In me you have infused
A portion of your timeless mind
Though I cannot contain all your thoughts.
Your ways I cannot fully comprehend,
Yet now I have begun to understand
A little of your plan for all of us,
Just a little of what you want for me.


## 10.  *WHAT IS TIME FOR YOU?*

The sun and the moon
And the planets,
And the stars, distant suns,
Move into place in their
Myriad galaxies
At your behest,
Orbiting around you

In the limitless expanse
Of your vast universe,
Giant pinwheels gyrating
Through timeless tunnels,
Channels of eons and chronons,
Microseconds and milliseconds.

For what is time for you?
You are the same today,
Yesterday and forever.
A thousand years is one day,
One day a thousand years for you.
And what is a light year?
A million light years?
That was yesterday.
Another million light years?
That would be tomorrow.

Today is but a moment for you
Streaking through the vacuum of space
At the fantastic speed of light,
Yet still unable to gird your heart,
Nor plumb the depths of your spirit.
Our mightiest radio telescopes,
Feeling the pulse of your universe,
Peering through the darkness
Jeweled by billions of diamonds
Emitting fire and brilliance
Through their billion years,
Can only hear the loudest whispers
Of your eternal breath.

## 11.  *THE GHETTOS OF OUR MINDS*

We, in our smugness and our self-will,
Can only listen to the black holes
Of our scientific minds
Long sequestered from your thinking,
Tinkering with the computerized toys
Of our logic, our philosophies,
Our organized theories.

We make the quantum leap
Out of the ghettos of our minds
And range over the archipelagos of time,
Your unrecorded time, your timeless time,
Before time was ever time.

And now at last on the threshold of knowledge,
We begin to make our guesstimates,
Propounding theories from speculations
That probably the whole scenario
Is not yours,
But purely a product of accident,
A colossal chance.

Chance? Accident?
The laugh is on us.
Forgive our folly.
Preempt the magnitude of our ignorance
With the simplicity of your mercy.

## 12.   *ISLANDS IN SPACE*

But I say, Father,
It is all your handiwork.
Though indeed you need no hands
To do your work.
Your will is enough
To make us alive and walk.

And because you took us out
Of our childhood ghettos, to view
Your countless islands in space
I now realize where I am
In your eternal plan.

## 13. *GODBLOOD DRAINED, LOVING TO DEATHPOINT*

Though indeed but a speck of dust,
From dust you formed me,
A grain of sand upon the shores
Of time and space,
I know you love me
As I am, ungainly as I am,
Loving me, this unlovable self
To deathpoint, draining
Godblood of your son
To slake our thirst for living water,
To wash singuilt from our flesh,
That it might become pure bread
For fellow pilgrims
Homeward bound to you.
But the mystic marvel is not only
That you have saved us,
Unredeemable as we were, but
You resurrected us to new life

When we were dead as dry bones,
And gave us each a portion
Of your spirit,
Making the human divine,
Infusing Godlife in us
To make us Godlike for life.


## 14.  *ON DEATH'S CROSSBAR, REBIRTH*


As if these were not enough,
You've made Jesus our brother.
A brother in truth who took on himself
The shape, the bones, the weakness
Of our flesh, answering for us
At the crossbar
With love and mercy,
Accepting whiplash and scorn,
Rejection and thorn,
Shorn of dignity and divinity,
That we might be born
Anew to you.

Your love has mitigated all
The pain of our rebirth,
And death has been mocked
to death in death.
Indeed you found us all guilty,
But your verdict was mercy;
And you've sentenced us all
To eternal life with you.

## 15. *TREMENDOUS LOVER INDWELLING*

And so today, this poem within me
Aching for release, this song,
This puny paean, my little hymn
Of thanksgiving I send upward,
Loveward where love is,
Heartward where the great
Heart of love resides
In supreme majesty
And pure, simple glory,
Unspoiled by the billion years
Of creative power to summon
Us to live and die and live again.

All along, deep within me,
While I gazed upwards in hope,
You, my self-effacing Father,
Always seeking me, but hiding from me,
Sent your spirit dwelling in me,
Temple for your tremendous love.

# CIRILO F. BAUTISTA

## THE FOURTEEN STATIONS OF THE CROSS

### I. *JESUS BEFORE PONTIUS PILATE*

*The cosmic and human drama as described in the Bible is an interplay between two partners playing against each other: Aleph, intermittent life-death, unfathomable, timeless mystery evading all mental grasp, and Yod, its projection into the time-space continuum, which is its antinomy.*
—Carlo Suarés, **The Cipher of Genesis**


The Power That Be In Whom Nothing Is False,
how can tinsel and tonsure twist His tongue?
The kangaroos that congregate in this court
earn my anger but I do not share their rues—          1

what use is Qabbala or palaver,
incense or wax or temple supplication,
when silence disembowels one's god? To say
of this nationhood it is a nation          2

of hoods is to hoist helicons in the square,
is to hoodwink none of the witches that bite
gold to test its worth, is to insure one's
dragomen a mile long, dragging his grave robe          3

by horses' feet. The termagants in the street
will terminate bony beatitudes,
having no shares in desert condominiums,
nor will the minimum premium the scribes          4

47

prescribe on scapulars erase the items
on this man's card. God or no God? If I had
all the elephants of Rome I would dare him
turn their tails to pyrotechnics to prove his                    5

texts; but in a country where rubble is rex
and rabbits rub butter on the revenue
nothing can renew a fallen spine, be it
of cosmos or of comedy. Twenty                                   6

inchlings with ideograms in their intestines,
testing by circus the bolts of miracles,
cannot invent the glyptics for his gloom,
even as now his beard is an epitaph                              7

for a ten-day lux at the lupercal.
God or no God? Were I to break him at
the wheels I will not discover the code
of his chord, the moony parables he spread                      8

like mandrake in the wind; were I to make
him a temple priest I would not resist
his magic, nor would the quick and the sick
amongst us, nor would the ash and candlestick                   9

in the dark. Son of Moses, what is Truth?
A clap-trap for the brain? A bastard child?
Create the cipher, create the symbol,
now, at once, before the water drowns my hands!                 10

## II. *JESUS RECEIVES THE CROSS*

*Every nation which had an astronomical symbol . . . held the
cross in the highest reverence, for it was the geometrical basis of the
religious symbolism of their avatars. . . .*
—H. P. Blavatsky, **Isis Unveiled**
*The journey of a thousand miles begins with one step.*
—Lao Tzu, **Tao Te Ching**


Blood in the moon is blood in the mind: the tic
in the hangman's hand is toxic in Pilate's
speech, for each to each descends the lunar
parables—the prick in the chasuble                                 1


and the pain in the foot. Stone on stone he will
scrape his bone he will break the rhyme of his song
he will ride the night mares in the dust. To think
at last this woody invention would invert                          2


his pineal gland and place his third eye in
his jaws is moral jugglery, though you can
jingle jubilees and he will not jumble
the tunes, his ears being optic. Blood in                          3


the mind is blood on the cross, a loss of
lemon and turpentine, a demon in wine
his sweat will not exorcise nor price with
lotus in the slaughterhouse. Timber will be                        4


his anadem, INRI his anagram.
Can the lilies of the valley and the white
birds of the sky support his pain? Priest or
no priest, God or no God, he will gobble                           5


garbage for lunch. All men that have loved him,
all men that he has loved, praise him no more,
their sandals preach no more, they are bantam;
their silence weighs on this wood and on all                       6

the timber in the universe, they will not
share his garbage. Occultic scripts he sees
in the woody load where the rabble sees
the blood, oh, so cross-eyed he is, trading                    7

folktales with the fish and biting pieces
of the moon, so much does he chatter from
the corner of his mouth. No viol or
mandolin drowns his moans as his shoulder                    8

scrapes the wood, as his blood rubs the wood, and
his shadow is hot with loneliness. Ten
thousand elephants pushing the plexus
of this planet to a blacksmith's pit will not                    9

crack his cross, nor clip his ticket inside
the circus maximus. Oh, this crooked
philosopher, this fiery fictioneer!
His grief covers the city like leprosy.                    10


## III.  *JESUS FALLS*

*The idea that man has been created in the image of God leads
not only to the concept of man's equality with God, or even freedom
from God, it also leads to a central humanist conviction that every
man carries within himself all of humanity.*
>                    —Erich Fromm, **You Shall Be As Gods**

*The four-dimensional body is the infinite number of three-
dimensional bodies. That is, the four-dimensional body is the in-
finite number of moments of existence of the three-dimenstional
one—its states and positions.*
>                    —P. D. Ouspensky, **Tertium Organum**

A mathematical bondage, a logic
rigmarole, that the world should compute its
repute by this man's bones! Phthisic, albeit
photic, what phospor has he that can melt                    1

the salt in phylacteries? Now that his
pinion is a cross, now that his pillow
is a cross, now that his zero is a cross,
now that his hero is a cross, magic                          2

will not stick electric in his brain. None
in his mystic clique has courage to cluck
his parables, seeing his paradigm
shattered by the vocal throng throwing spears                3

at his back. To postulate loneliness
as the condition for grace—Joshua,
Moses, Melchizedek, each with his own
sarcoma, each with his own sarcophagus—                      4

scratches merely the scapulary. But of
the moony mongerings, the scallop shell,
as it were, that stretch the road under his
sandals, scandals will not scare. So, as he                  5

drags his leprosy across the square and
drowns with sweat his bloody crown, he moves in
his mind the digits of a formula:
where X is the mace of a matchbox throne,                    6

and thorns the headgear of gallantry, the sum
priesthood takes is prophylactic, equal
to apocryphal. He is a moving
zero, then, an ambulation without                            7

map, selling breadcrumbs for a broken god.
He did commerce with cornstalk in caves, counting
sheep and shibboleths to annotate his
income tax, but relax his bloodstream his god                8

will not now as his knees scrape the universe
and his shoulders bend under the wood. What could
condemn his Bethlehem to the formula
antique that blinded Isis and locked the lakes                    9


of Egypt? God or no God, priest or no priest,
what princelings ride his back to preserve their boon?
One man against the books, one leprous digit,
bleeding for a world without wax nor flowers.                    10



## IV.  *JESUS MEETS HIS MOTHER*

*An occult tradition suggests that She also attained to Adeptship,
either in that life or later, and She is said to have chosen that one
of the seven paths which takes the Adept into the Deva Kingdom.*
                    —Geoffrey Hodson, **The Soul's Awakening**


*Hawthorn is called Crataegus oxyacantha, from the Greek
kratos, which means hardness of wood; oxus, which is sharp, and
akantha which is thorn. It attains to a height of about thirty feet
and lives to a great age. The hawthorn was regarded as sacred by
the English country villagers during the Middle Ages, probably from
the tradition that it furnished Christ's Crown of Thorns.*
                    —Paul Twitchell, **Herbs, the Magic Healers**



Mother of Water, Queen of Leprosy,
she has no song or sorcery to ease
his pain; she has only melancholy
that pushes the thorny bush down his brows,                    1


she whose ancestry is the ark. She has no
need for trinkets to be glad, nor trances
to trace the end of his wounds; how she knows
the politics, the palaver! Her heart                    2

is a catacomb already, though he still
drags his blood across the dust. Queen of Rust,
Graceless Grex, hang Qabbala round your neck
and break the code of Jonah and Joshua                    3

with the twelve stones, of Hermes Trismegistus
with snakes, of David in his tower,
Solomon with his lemon, Peter in Rome.
They had no home to formalize their grief,                4

no desert dune or palm leaf proclaimed their
passage. And he, in an age of witchery,
carries his destiny on his back. Being
mother of all burning ships, her womb defined            5

her son's decline, but now, being also
a woman, she weakens at his faltering
steps. And when their eyes meet this eternal
moment—when he sees a woman and she                       6

the Light—her brain clicks his catalogue: born
in a manger, condemned to the cross. Between
the terminals of this biography are
an ashram in Tibet, a temple in                          7

India, and a bantam that cackled three
times. For she to him is more than a mother;
in the formula antique, her sorrow
is his sword, her constancy his grace; she is            8

the crux of his cortex, the corona
of his cares. Their meeting is a meeting
of two worlds divided by a sign she
cannot divine. Perhaps of Amalek                         9

it is, who sold his birthright for pottage,
and Amalekites these are who sold her son
for a joke: thirty pieces of silver
turn their two worlds into a black-eyed witch.           10

## V.  *JESUS IS HELPED BY THE CYRENEAN*

*To him who overcomes . . . I will give him a white stone, and on
the stone a new name written, which no one knows except he who
receives it.*

**—Revelation**

*The Church is never a body, never an assembly. An individual
soul becomes aware that it has taken that Head, that Son, that Man
even, to be the intermediator. That is the Church. . . . What readest
thou? "Upon this I will build my church." What church? . . . Here ye
may find the answer again to many of those questions concerning
the Spirit, the Church, the Holy Force that manifests by the attuning
of the individual, though it may be for a moment.*

—Edgar Cayce, in Krajenke's
**Man Crowned King: The Divine Drama Unfolds**

Whether they be witches or warlocks who choke
his likeness in rags, or royal inchlings
with itches in their pocket, this fictioneer
is a fool! The heaven he built from the rocks　　　　　　　1

of his mind remains unbought, for who would buy
a graveyard for his greed? Who would barter
his coffer for a promise of wings? "All
for Israel," he cried, wishing legions　　　　　　　2

protected his parables. Israel!
Is Rachel a toxin? Is totem worser
than Opium? Can anything good come
from Israel? Down by the temple gate　　　　　　　3

the lepers lick their wounds, down by the tinder
box the leopards lick their meat—neither would die
for Israel! And this son of David,
this corner-stone of Israel, half-limping　　　　　　　4

54

across the universe, has lost the map
to his heaven! The stallion prances in
the weeds and has no oat to chew! The few
he led by the nose with hokus-pokus                          5

of levitation and multiplying fish
have betrayed him, afraid of cross-sticks on
the hill. Oh, the strife for this tinkling tin
of a life! All you gods of Israel, where                     6

is your goat? Bring a rain of iron, gold,
brass, silk and wine to signify your wrath!
Bring worms and serpents and lice and locusts!
Let them pay the price! To them who are wise,               7

be unforgiving! To them who are living,
be assassin! Be torture! Be obscene!
Support the spine of your house even as now
I support it, the universe with it,                          8

the weight and height of anger and doom. God
or no God, priest or no priest, rosemary
will not bloom in his blood, neither will spiders;
in the night most black only the raven                      9

will raise his dirge, and none of the scholars
who sneer at his ancestry will inscribe
his name for the census. The devil on us
if his maxims mix their sting on his tomb!                   10

## VI.  *JESUS MEETS VERONICA*



*Now I shall tell thee of the end of wisdom. When a man knows
this he goes beyond death. It is Brahman, beginningless, supreme:
beyond what is and beyond what is not.*

—**Bhagavad Gita**

*And how shall you punish those whose remorse is already
greater than their misdeeds? Is not remorse the justice which is ad-
ministered by that very law which you would fain serve?*

—Kahlil Gibran, **The Prophet**

The devil on us if his maxims dance
on his tomb! A jig in the jugular vein
for the juice of martyrdom does not insure
us against prophets and pestilence, nor                           1

would a thousand bantams bar these Christmen
from the cave. The halo and the stave he
struck us with melted in our jest, the test
he put us to rotted with his fish, yet                            2

I cannot forget that woman's look, the one
with blackbirds in her eyes, her face the canvas
of a phantom caravan—the look of a
sister and a mistress combined, a flaming,                        3

electric look! What is she? Who forsook
her on this land? In a crowd of indigenes
she is gold; in a crowd of blue virgins
she is old—a leper without disease,                               4

a dancetune only mongers can dance!
The blackbirds carry her tomb and her nightgown
down the rude gorges of greed and I amongst
the most rabid, the most raucous, saying                          5

56

with lancets in my eyes, "Leave, leave this man
alone! DO not meddle with his bone! Do not
provoke the stars!" But she stands rooted to
her faith in mandrakes and magicians, deaf                    6


to all but the call of calculus in
her veil: though not an idiot, a fool to wave
cloth in the wind to court salvation! Ayy,
Veronique of the Essenes! Veronique                          7


of the catacombs! What miracle will
your Hermes Trismegistus or this bloody
Jesus create to lessen the darkness
of your days? Will his touchstone terminate                  8


the wait for the Second Sun? Bah, an ass
in Sinai is an ass in Rome! That sun,
or this sun, can no more clip its zodiac
·than an ass its parentage. What usage                       9


has your veil with his three faces when the jeer
of the crowd dazes your brain? God or idiot,
prophet or zealot, he will need galactic
props to support the pieces of his pride!                    10


## VII.  *JESUS FALLS AGAIN*

*Giorgio Piccardi, Professor of Geophysics at Florence, in a bril-
liant series of experiments has proved that the methodology of re-
search based on the Principle of Carnot is false. . . . The Earth gyrates
around the sun which moves through space toward the constella-
tion of Sagittarius. The Earth thus moves in a spiral trajectory cross-
ing lines of force created by the Milky Way, whose galactic field in
motion is influenced by all the moving matter and energy in the
universe. Each human being is a concretion of electrical energy.*
—W. Raymond Drake, **Gods and Spacemen in the Ancient East**

To support the particulars of one's pride,
to press one's suit for martyrdom—is this not
apostacy? Granting he is mad, granting
he has had the devil's inspiration—                          1

must not his very church castigate him?
His parables are untenable, being
paroxysms of the mind, and would convince
only the contumely. Thus, I reject                           2

his posturing for a kingship that will
never come. While on the stone his blood runs dry,
and the scarecrows cackle in the noonday sky,
what is the substance of his talk? This alone:               3

that suffering is father to the lilies,
as if singing fish and jumping bread were not
enough, as if the coffers of Rome could be
subverted by a loom; this alone: that sex                    4

electrifies the soul, and sperm weakens
the Christian tongue, as if a clan of
disembodied Jews could juggle his death
away! The premises, the promises                             5

of his paradise perpetuate the lies
prophets feed on, so, when all his inchlings
betrayed his trust, he faced his judges with
nothing but a sweaty loin. Recall his                        6

logic: when asked if he was Christ, he replied—
"Thou hast said it." A plastic sophistry,
if I am asked, but a crafty one; for, if
indeed he is Christ, the premise assumes it,                 7

and, if he is not, no earthly proof can
reflect it! Three pounds of flax and olive oil
cut him from the wellspring of Rome, and the cross
returns his lie. Thirty pieces of silver          ·         8

broke his syllogism—not mysticism
or such—whose tinkle had seductive speech
for his crooked saints. Neither statesman nor
scholar, he needs carrion color to redeem          9

his name. No wonder, as he falls the second
time, he falls alone, the chime in his bone
the hangman's joy. Exit the devil's cow.
Good-bye. No argument can save him now.       10


## VIII. *JESUS SPEAKS TO THE WEEPING WOMEN*

*By having compassion for the helpless one, man begins to
develop love for his brother; and in his love for himself he also loves
the one who is in need of help, the frail, insecure human being.*
> —Erich Fromm, **The Art of Loving**


*Orchids in Spring and chrysanthemums in Autumn:
so it shall go on till the end of time.*
> —Chu Yuan, "The Nine Songs"


Women with dark teeth, women with missing teeth,
women with the wounds of ages on your back,
I wipe away your tears. Weep not, for though
nothing can save me, I say unto you          1

no king nor henchman to this day has killed me
as they will kill me in the coming years.
I do not say, then, "My bones ache." I do not
say, then, "Revenge on the bastards!" Even as      2

I bleed now, hundreds like me in Venus,
Jupiter, in all the other planets,
shed this very blood in a very like
journey. Why then must I seek the comfort                3

of my bones? Why then must I visit evil
on the enemy? Comfort never will come
to me or my brothers, and the enemy
is only the other side of my face. If                    4

the bullfrog can make of mud a habitat,
and raise a clean song amidst darkness, so
can you, daughters of Israel, construct
from sorrow a joyous chant to lighten                    5

this burden. Scrape the beeswax from your eyes
and see me as I am: a cornered rat,
an ultimate fool rattling bronze coins at
the gods. My squeak and flummery will not               6

feed the lilies nor castrate the ox, but
in Egypt and Tibet they will shake temple
bells, closing the seventh chakra: you have
drunk of my blood and eaten of my flesh—                7

were they any better than your own? Why then
do you weep for a common sinner? Contain
the winner of my flesh in the ballad
of your blight, think of me tonight as you              8

break bread, so that even as you weep for me
I shall smile at my cowardice. All this,
this grab at the windy crown is pig's dung
on Roman history, and I shall smile                     9

at my cowardice. Women of the tombs,
what if I fall a million times? Will your bone
weep for me as you weep now? Or will you say,
"The idiot! Why does he not leave us alone?"            10

## IX.  *JESUS FALLS THE THIRD TIME*

*The world being as large as it is, it is probably necessary every
now and then to mark time culturally for a thousand years or so.
And this is what seems to have happened in the single cycle of which
we have historical knowledge. The Roman genius for organization
and the influence of a supernaturally enforced—and therefore more
easily comprehensible—system of Christianity were necessary to
bring the hordes of sans-culottes of the European forests slowly to
the point where, in two thousand years, they might continue where
the Greeks left off.*
—Hans Zinsser, Rats, Lice and History

I told them they would not listen—"Leave all
that is well enough alone, Rome does not care,
the Essenes do not care. Why rattle
the rocks with a skeleton?" But they went on      1

to seduce blood on the mountain with bits
of rhetorics and black magic and the sky
was heavy with darkness. When first I heard
that he must hang I thought at last the Devil      2

had caught up with him so much had he spoken
with sugar in his tongue yet offered us
nothing but blisters and sweat! Oh, I thought,
remembering the stories told about him,      3

I thought, well, he had made his cross and he
must hang, and neither the lutes of Lebanon
nor the dunes of Africa could hide his guilt,
the vineyards of Polonius would not wither      4

with his death. Like leprosy we swarm the streets
to see him scrape his bone, as last night with
a kiss we ended commerce with his soul.
Oh, what a bastard he is! All those tortures      5

61

got from him was "Peace!", as if one could live
on petals of roses. I wonder
when the scriveners shall have tallied the books
and the eunuchs closed the palace gates,                            6

and the rock reclined against the cave, what shall
we have by way of emblem for this so-called
victory? Will he whom we shall hang be flung
to the wolves? Or will his disembowelled                            7

legion raise his religion above our head?
I fear starcraft and bonecraft will not save
this country, my country, till his body is
given the rites. . . . And now as he embraces                       8

the dust a third time I fear his blood will be
on our skull! I fear for our men and women,
I fear the magic in his name! The shame
this day smears on our record will return                           9

dung on our plates and constrict our bowels!
The wheels are turning, my beloved killers,
beware! Turn your ears to my toothless words,
I, an old man, without beard or mistresses. . . .                  10


## X.  *JESUS IS STRIPPED*

*The very existence of science is a witness to the existence of a
cosmic order.*

> —Henri-L. Mieville, **Vers une philosophie de l'esprit**

*The wrathful deities represent hope, and the peaceful deities rep-
resent fear. Fear in the sense of irritation, because the ego cannot
manipulate them in any way; they are utterly invincible, they never
fight back. The hopeful quality of wrathful energy is hope in the sense
of perpetua l creative situation, seen as it really is, as a basic neutral*

*energy which continues constantly, belonging neither to good nor
bad.*


—Chogyam Trungpa, Rinpoche, commentary
to **The Tibetan Book of the Dead**

How much for a pound of this flesh, how much
for a cup of this blood? Come on, come around
for The Greatest Show of the Roman Empire!
Presenting, fresh from his tour of the hills          1

of Galilee and the caves of Egypt,
having traversed a hundred miles to talk
to the birds and the fish, in authentic
living color—and odor—Jesus the King!          2

Observe his hair: ten thousand birds and lice
have nestled in his hair and have listened
to the ticking of his brain; they know this hair,
when boiled or greased, is an effective charm          3

against leprosy and the evil eye:
how much am I bid for his hair? Observe
his clothes: reeking with the filth of India
and Bethlehem, what can rebut its occult          4

pedigree? To some degree the aura
of his loins and armpits is the corona
of our despair, for the hoax it engenders
might perpetuate his flock! What do you see          5

in the holes of his shirt? Do not the perfumes
of Arabia and the sweet sweat of Tibet
emanate therefrom? What are the scents of Rome
compared to these? How much am I bid for his          6

clothes? Observe his sandals: many scandals
they have spread in this land, among the lepers
and the pharisees, among the prostitutes
and scums; the straps and soles have befouled the most          7

holy soil of Caesar; they will recline
in a temple by the Ganga, to be
adored by cows and monkeys, if at all.
How much am I bid for these sandals? Observe          8

the system of his bones; observe the noble
curve of his chin, the shoulder joints sticking out
but firm, the rib-cage, the knee-caps, the heels—
they will purge the ghosts in any pantheon—          9

how much am I bid for this skeleton?
Bring out your money, shout me your bid, our
sale will end all sales in this part of Rome!
Buy your souvenirs now and brighten your home!          10


## XI.  *JESUS IS NAILED TO THE CROSS*

*The Christians wish to replace our beautiful legends with the police record of a reforming rabbi. Out of this unlikely material they hope to make a final synthesis of all the religions ever known. They now appropriate our feast days. They transform local deities into saints. They borrow from our mystery rites, particularly those of Mithras. The priests of Mithras are called "fathers." So the Christians call their priests "fathers." They even imitate the tonsure, hoping to impress new converts with familiar trappings of an older cult.*

—Maximus, in Gore Vidal's **Julian**


Why should I, of all the thousand idiots
in Arimathea, be chosen for this
despicable job? I keep the fire of
Mithras burning with goat blood and chicken blood,          1

Asklepios blesses my boils—what signals
clobbered me to cross my fate with this Jew's?
King of kings, he calls himself, The Light of Judah,
with his feet in the stars and his hands upon          2

the seas—well, with rusty nails I nullify
the rhythm of his runes, I who have no
magic, his limbs will flap no more to trick us
with levitation or multiplying          3

fishes, his words will wither in the sun.
"Let the duality of things work for you,"
he preached, "if the storm sends you a flood, build
a boat." So, if you be hungry, dine with          4

the Devil? No sooner had he left hammer
and chisel for the fishnets of Galilee
than the ravens covered with their wings his
graceful geography. Reduced to a pin          5

head, his kingdom crumbled with a kiss. So
why was I marked to meddle with this wreck?
God or no God, his blood will be on my name,
it will flow under my door and over          6

my bed to smear the gold boxes of my dreams,
to drown the roses in my runes, even as
now it spurts on my gown and spatters my face!
O prophet Zarathustra, O divine          7

Zeus, Hades, and Helios, hear the voice
of one in the dark: I charge you, by the souls
of my ancestors, by the tallows in
our temples, at this moment, to shut your          8

Judgment Book: do not record this infamy:
do not reckon my fate with this man's fault:
do not destroy the silver in my house:
he is not the measure of my manhood,          9

nor I of his ministry! This mystery
grips me like a plague. I do not understand
why three nails and a fool's blood should obstruct
my fruity passage into Mithras' land. . . .                         10


## XII.  *JESUS DIES*

*The idea of secrecy, of being closed up and hermetically sealed,
is included in that of mystery. . . . The root of the words mystery,
mystic, mysticism, and myth is the same. The Sanskrit word 'mus'
means to act in a hidden way, privily, in secret. Myths borrow from
among the data, images and symbols of sense the means by which
they attempt to express, as far as they can, the inexpressible.*
—Adolphe Ferriere, Psychological Types<br>and the Stages of Man's Development

*Death is the state from which resuscitation of the body as a
whole is impossible by currently known means.*
—A. S. Parkes, quoted in The Prospects of Immortality


So, it is ended . . . And so, it is begun . . .
From one terminus of pain to the other.
Like the streets of cancer. To have cancelled
the cosmic convulsions, to have checked the                         1


lunar clock—only to dangle from a
cross-stick on a hill? Why must your history
be inscribed with my blood? Each drop that shapes
the letter burns with the anger in my                               2


bowels . . . All or nothing, you said, and sent me
to sell the Good News . . . No funds, no chariots,
no armies, I was to vanquish ten thousand gods
with the Good News! I'll give you Israel,                           3


66

you said . . . Israel! Buried in dung heaps,
renounced by her fathers, a leper with
festering sores—that is your Israel!
All that she was, all that she ever will be,                4

will not buy raiments for my flesh . . . and her tricks
with palm leaves that made Bethlehem a widow
and Jerusalem a whore will not roll
the rock-door from my tomb . . . Such as I am              5

I am—a dogsbody craving for the cup
you never filled and the bread you never broke,
all for Israel! I spit on Israel!
Her sons shall not suck of my flame nor her               6

daughters of my grace . . . but I shall crush the seeds
in their loins till they be a nation of
hags and scarecrows . . . when I return. One by one
they shall wilt by the wayside, the bride with            7

the bridegroom, the young with the old, the quick
with the cold . . . till the air groans with the stench
of decay! No more jasmine in my mouth . . .
nor amber in my ears when I return!                       8

No larkspur in the Spring! No wood in Winter!
No more miracles! Pain has drained the occult
in my soul . . . and no wedding or dead child
can make me flick my fingers in magic. . . .             9

So it is ended . . . And so it is begun . . .
From womb to cross, written in blood, your will.
The snakes and vultures await the Good News. . . .
The Good News hangs, a lean corpse on a hill. . . .      10

## XIII.  *JESUS IS UNFASTENED FROM THE CROSS*



Ever so gently, sons of Israel!
Do not break the dream in his brain! Do not
pull his flesh against the nails! Lower him
ever so gently so his blood does not stain                    1

his landscape of sleep. Son of David, dream
of this: a house of water, with shell roof
and sapphire door, gleaming in the rise and fall
of the waves; inside, your wounded heart pounding                    2

in tune with the universe, emitting
flames that burn the wicked! And around you,
over and beyond you, legions of angels
bearing you on silent wheels! And as they                    3

praise your parables, their wings smoothen the waves!
Silence upon silence crown you with a
layer of light! O Son of David, Lord
of the Seven Ladders, forget the pain                    4

in your soul, dream of this! Gently, gently,
daughters of Galilee, wash his wounds with
sacred oil, wipe his sweat with sacred satin,
lay his bones on the grass. His sorrow will pass,                    5

but the scribes and Pharisees and hypocrites
who tithe mint, dill, and cummin and omit
justice and mercy and faith, will wallow
in eternal sadness. Gently, pour perfume                    6

on his hair, rub it on his eyes and skin,
prepare his body. For did he not say,
"Jerusalem! Jerusalem! Murdering
the prophets and stoning those sent to you! How          7

often have I wanted to gather your
children but you were unwilling; see, your house
is forsaken!" Did he not say, "I will
send you prophets and sages and scribes, some          8

of whom you will kill and crucify, so that
there may come upon you all the righteous
blood that has been shed on earth!" Let his blood
be clean for the Second Coming. Now, daughters,          9

change his rags with this sweet winding sheet, white
against the darkness of this day. Wrap him
tightly so the cloth warms him in the rock. . . .
Son of David, Lord of Light, farewell—good-night. . . .          10

## XIV.  *JESUS IS BURIED*

*For after death, as they say, the genius of each individual, to whom he belonged in life, leads him to a certain place in which the dead are gathered together, whence after judgment has been given they pass into the world below, following the guide, who is appointed to conduct them from this world to the other: and when they have there received their due and remained their time, another guide brings them back again after many revolutions of ages.*
       —Plato, **Phaedo**

*He lingers; such is the nature of the gods above.*
       —Euripedes, **Orestes**

My Lover is gone amongst the Lilies,
is walking in the Valley of Thorns:
Flames in his Ears, He would not hear the Horns
calling, "Come back! Put on your Armor and Shield!"	1

*Son of David, close not the Gate on Us!*
*Son of David, re-awaken our Wombs!*
*Son of David, place Lyrics in our Sleep!*
*Son of David, must we forever Weep?*	2

He is gone into the Waters rushing
to embrace the Seaweeds and the Fishes;
"Brothers," He says, "You have kept my Wishes,"
and his Tears tumble with the roaring Tide.	3

*Son of David, drown not our Fathers' Names!*
*Son of David, Baptize our Bodies again!*
*Son of David, place Lyrics in our Sleep!*
*Son of David, must we forever Weep?*	4

My Lover is gone into the Mountains
where Beasts and Fowls lick his festering Sores.
He blesses the Birds, the Rabbits, and the Boars.
The Moon swings down to re-arrange his Hair.	5

*Son of David, hide not your Heart in the Rocks!*
*Son of David, carve the Steps to your Soul!*
*Son of David, place Lyrics in our Sleep!*
*Son of David, must we forever Weep?*	6

My Lover is gone amongst the Dead in Hell
whom He comforts in brotherly Embrace.
They read the Promise of Joy in his Face
and their Tears shatter the Walls of the Cave.	7

*Son of David, remember us in our Grief!*
*Son of David, lift Darkness from our Head!*
*Son of David, place Lyrics in our Sleep!*
*Son of David, must we forever Weep?*	8

My Lover is gone to the House in the Skies
where Torch-trees and gold Larks announce his Name!
Enthroned, Purified, He reads the Book of Shame
to correct the Dark Deeds inscribed therein!                9

*Son of David, remember Israel!*
*Son of David, uncover her Children's Eyes!*
*Son of David, place Lyrics in our Sleep!*
*Son of David, must we forever Weep?*                10

Zambales-Quezon City: 1974-1977

## FRAGMENTS FROM THE JOURNAL
## OF OBISPO GREGORIO AGLIPAY

*The First Fragment*
**Antiphon**

Will God's hammer fall
if I throw my Roman pieties
        to the wind, like straw?

They are asking me

To risk the hammer of his wrath
        and turn to straw

What has been ordained
        as stone:

the rock of Peter
the crown in Rome

                        the
celibate throne that accepts
no empress because its keeper
is a fisherman

        wed to his fish.

An Italian fisherman
in the Mare Sinica

        Oh, how his hook
tethers my soul

                        the
line unbroken, guarded by bulls
heavy with Latin prose, this language
withered men in purple choose

                    to grace
their ark.

                    Ordained
in stone,

                    Woven into
cassock, surplice and robe,

in this robe
where my manhood lies
                        hidden
in folds.

                    By this altar
where I am made to fall

Penitent,

bidden to lie folded
like a turtle

                    in its shell.

                    Oh I am bound.

I am bound to the tree of Rome,
though it be neither cypress, poplar
                            nor oak.

                    stands limbed
and rooted all the same, clawed

To the sky: There is no way.

                    You must eat
of its bark. The tree of Rome
is the new she-wolf:

                    Come, suck its roots,
drink in the blood of Stephen Martyr,

be mothered.

                    For
in the beginning was the mother

                    who
clothed you in prayer, let the red
of her scapular flow across your chest,
led you by the hem of her brown
Franciscan skirt.

                    Look
at the man dying on the cross. See
how his mouth is open.

                    Deliver
your prayers to his open mouth, let
the smoke from your candles waft into
his open

                    Mouth.

The open mouth does not speak.

The first lessons flow from your mother,
Like the newborn

                    they scream
in your mind. Why is the mouth of God

open?

                              Who
has heard him scream?
The first lesson in pain is Jesus Christ
of the Open Mouth. Do not laugh.

Rome
tells us
        when to laugh,

when to cry. When to open
our mouths

                like crickets,
                        only at the appointed hours

                like lizards,
                        only at the appointed hours

For we must also kiss
                the ground.

Be quiet in church, see how your mother,
                                quiet,

walks like a snail
                her knees bent,

                her back bent,
                her veil
                        peaked,
                her eyes closed,
                her mouth closed,
                her lips
                        moving

in silent waves that
                crash
upon his ears.

He will bring down his hand
like a hammer

                    Oh his terror
is greater than your father's
                    His eyes
redder than the tip of your father's

                              cigar.

You are a nail

                              and
                              he
who carries the hammer of the Father
                    loves you.

He loves you
as he pounds you into
                    the roof
                    of his house.

He will have the top of your head
shaven and clean like a nail. He will offer you

                    up to his father
and say: receive this nail and make him holy,
breathe your spirit into this nail

                    and make him pure
                    because he has rust

in his soul.

Blessed Mother, protect my son.
Son,
        go kiss her navel
        cling to her waist.

        She
who carries no hammers
                is

the mother of all
who carry hammers
                all
who pound nails
into her son's house, all
                who
judge between the rusted
nail
        and the pure nail.

                        Oh
how I scream in the dreams of my sleep,
he is coming down, Mother, with a net in his hands:

I am a fisherman still, come to my net.

                                Oh
I dream in the sea of my sleep

                                Oh
I drown in the arms of his long net

He takes me into his Open Mouth
                        and

I drown.

                They are asking me,
poor fool, they are asking me to cast my
Roman pieties
                        to the sea.

Like pebbles.

                Yet my Roman pieties
are not faceless.

                          All mothers
have faces, who says the first of these pieties
are faceless?

Who, like me, have not been ordained by their mothers?
                                              Who,
like me, have not been taken to church by their mothers?
                                              Who,
like me, have not been taken to see the Open Mouth of God?
                                              Who,
like me, have not been taught that the mouth lies open?
                                              Who,
like me, have not been taught that the Open Mouth leads

to a gullet
              that leads to Rome?

I am bound to the tree of Rome.

I am bound to the tree of Rome:
I climb its trunk and feel
                          how wide my God is
and how painfully he scratches my knees.

                                        The
first lesson is pain. That is why God
has a hammer.

                              You
are a nail.

                                        The
second lesson is more pain. That is why God
has a net of many hands.

                              You
must drown.

                                        The
third lesson is death. That is why God
has an Open Mouth.

You

must die with your mouth open. The agony of
your dying is stuck in your throat.

Like a fishbone.

*The Second Fragment*
**Sea, Fish, Net and Gull**

Sea

                              whose bottoms
hold truth for the fisherman's arms, where
eternity's prefigured
                         by waves,
is home for the fisherman, home for his net:

                         Why
is his church not built on the sea? Where fish
may go to pray, sing bubbles, wave their fins,

Alleluia! Alleluia!

Rome has, alas, no seas, no bounty of fish
for its nets, only stones

                     to cobble its roads.
Can there be truth without fish? What is eternity
without the sea?

The sea celestial, aha, the sea celestial, aye,
there's the rub
                         in
the papal tub. Rome is the fisherman,
          Rome is the sea, Rome the net

that stretches over all who've tasted water,
been creamed by salt in the name of Rome's Father,
Rome's Son and Rome's Holy Spirit hovering
                                        like
a hungry gull.

Is it he who turns from fisherman to gull, who flies?

Has he flown?
Why are we his only fish


                                        in
Asia's belly?

The Spanish commission, perhaps gull, perhaps galleon,
salvation from the cowls of Spanish friars, the cowls

                        whose tips are
like hungry beaks that hover over the fish of these islands:

Amen to you natives, amen to you fish, amen to you brown

                        like the earth.

Some instructions:

Before reaching these shores, Urdaneta, make sure your frailes
turn

                to gulls.

On board ship, as master gull, you must make sure that this office
is clear to them:

                        Rome's Spirit hovers
                        like a hungry gull.
                            You
                        must be as hungry.
                        For only a hungry gull
                        catches fish.

The fish of these islands swim at the bidding of master fishes.
Your eyes must be sharp as you hover, for unless the master fish
is safe in the beak

                                                        all else
is lost. His family scatters to seek other masters, for the fish

of these islands live as slaves. They are born to follow a master
                                                        fish.

You will know a master fish by the manner in which

                                        he greets you.

                                        He will bring you
shells, clams and seaweeds and invite you to feast.Hewill have the
females of his fishold gather in circles round as your eyes and he will
bid them dance to the rhythm of the waves. You will know him by
what he does, for he alone will be doing the bidding.

He alone

will be able to look at you in the eye, for he                alone

is capable of seeing,                                            has

the eye.

                To catch the master fish
                your gulls must be instructed
                to abstain from feasting
                and to counter the dance
                with one
                        of their own:

By flying high above the waves, in circles, and if the female fish go
clockwise, by going counterclockwise, beating their wings twice as
fast as the female fish; but if they see the female fish go counterclock-
wise, they must reverse their motion and beat their wings twice as
slow.

The dance in the air will sunder the dance in the sea
and the warrior fish will not know what to do when your beaks
pounce upon the confused master.

      Secure between your beaks
      take your master fish up
           in the air.
      Swoop down three times and
      dip its head        in
      the water. And on the fourth
      swoop release him and let him
      fall.

Do the same to the other fish, Urdaneta, but do not have your gulled
friars take them as high in the air.           Respect
hierarchy,

      even among the fish. Even Rome
      and (shudder if you dare forget)
      Spain have their master fishes.

These facts are drawn
from history's nets:

      His father has parted the sea
      His mother been made its queen

      He has walked upon it, calmed a storm
                above it

      And he has multiplied fish
             upon land.

Now with Spanish nets, draw them in docile and draw them in
fresh, their eyes wet           their fins wet

      their scales heavy with knowledge of the sea,
      truths of the deep blue waters, insights

sharp as chipped coral, heavy with the profundity
that only tides can unveil:
                              The most obvious is the most real.

Take the fisherman who bathes
in sea water, whose hair and limbs
              are coated
              with seawater,
              who smells
              of the sea;

is he not more real                                    to the fish?

       But more real must be more obvious.

To be more real, one must go

                              beyond bathing,
Must   sprout   fins,   yes,   must   sprout   fins!

              Send word to every galleon,
              post notice in every Mexican port:

                              all
              who sail cowled must first be fitted

              with fins.

Or seahorse tails. And whether it be fins or tails, one each
for every gospel. Four to each friar. And if his nose be long
and hooked, then three only                            for

              that can be John's gospel:
              the revelation revealed

as a beak. Indeed, the long-nosed friars will have no problems

with conversion                              or conversation

To the fish they need only say:
Come to us, cursed without noses,
let our magic work on your curse.

                              Take
the Roman formula: bow to the Pope
and his friars.

                            · Take
the Spanish formula: bow to the King
and his friars.

                              And
all will be well with your sea.
                                    Friar,

part the sea at will: In doctrine there is
                  the strength of whales and if
                                    you believe,
                  a strength greater than that
                                    of all whales.

For what are whales but larger fish?

Part the sea. Cut it in half like a woman's garment. Be strong.

                                                    Rip it apart.

What power stays your hands?                          The power

of Rome's chrism                                          is in

the palms                                          of your hands


Chrism is oil

                  and oil rises
                  to the forehead
                    of any sea.                          You will not

84

go down to the deep.                                        You will

                    rise

                    rise

          to the forehead
          of the sea.

          There will be

                              no drowning here,
                              no drowning here.

From the sea's forehead you will call out to the fish:

                              "Come,
                              rise,
                              come
                              forth"

And people his mind.

Further instructions:

                    Teach them how it is
                              to wail

                    Teach them how it is
                              to wail

               in the deep.

                    Teach them how it is
                         to cry

                    Teach them how it is
                         to cry

               in water.

For you were brown before we came and will be brown forever-
more: that is nothing to grieve about. Rather grieve over the days
before we came for the brown fish is nothing without the white, is
nothing without the cowled white, is nothing without the cowled
white nets.

>           So heretofore
>           all generations before you
>           were cursed for their brownness:

    Father, grandfather and
                        great-grandfather
                                fish

    Mother, grandmother and
                        great-grandmother
                                fish

All
All were cursed for their brownness

All
All were doomed by their brownness

All
All were fated to nothing more after their brown
                                        death.

Grieve over that,
wail over that,
cry over that.

>           But that
>           was their fate

>           That
>           was their brown fate.

But blessed be your generation though it be brown
And blessed be the generations after you though they be brown
Blessed be all the brown generations to come

                                        for we are here
                                        with
                                        our white cowled nets

To take you farther than your brown deaths
To take you farther than your brown fates

                                        for our cowled
                                        white nets are as
                                        arms stretched

                                        to take you to
                                        our own seas

                                        to take you to

The seas of the white fish

                                        to take you to

The seas that know no death

                                        to take you to

The seas where fish do not wail
                nor weep
                nor grieve

                for there is nothing
                        nothing

                        to fear
                        to grieve about

Where there is white
Where there is white
Where there is white

                                          where white reigns
                                          and conquers over
                                                    brown
                                                      black
                                                    yellow

The seas, yea, the seas
and these are many

                    for there are seas
                                    with yellow fish

                    and there are seas
                                    with black fish

Seas just like yours
                    seas that we must visit

                    with our white cowled nets

                    for all the fish must be saved
                                        from death
                              must be brought
                                        beyond death

To seas without death
to the seas of the white fish

                    where there is no weeping
                    in the deep

                    where there are no tears

                    where there are no
                                    colors.

*The Third Fragment*
**The Tree of Rome**


The branches speak
                 in whispers:
Do not speak so close

to God in his heaven, it is not good
to have so many voices speak

                         to God
who hears only one voice. The tree of Rome
speaks only with one voice. Adonai.

A garden with only one tree.

I will swing from its branches
                         and fall.
How tall my God is, how I need him to reach
                                     the sky.

The tree of Rome is tall and taller even
than your father
                 who lifts you
                 up to his shoulders

and no farther.

                 For this reason you must give up
your father if you wish to climb the tree. Remember
your father only as a necessary piety,

                                     who
gave you seed and lifted you up to the first branch.

Rome assumes the rest, will feed you leaves

                 from the tree.

Leave your father to his own orchard,
he has chosen smaller trees, he has chosen not

                    to touch the sky.

Enough that he has fed you milk from his carabao
and rice from his field. You are no longer his

                    but Rome's.

The tree of Rome is a selfish tree, it towers
over mountains and mortal fathers, allows no one

                    the joy of the sky.

But you are privileged, for you the tree will always
                              be there.

Come and offer your prayer to the tree:
Be strong, tree, let your spirit flow
                              from root to crown,

preserve us from all storms, preserve us
from the tentacles of the sun, grant us peace

                    in your shade.

Under the shade of the Tree of Rome
walks another shadow          under

                              whose dark

fall other shadows.

Bring the natives of these islands to this dark night

                              Tell them
God does not dwell in fire but in shadow, not in light
but in dark.                              Black as

charcoal burnt from finest wood, black as the underside
of an old pot                                                                          is
                    his truth under shadow.

Leaves fall and are replaced, the shadow under this
tree stays, fixed firmly, final as roots.   Bring

the natives to this shadow, tell them all will be well
under this shadow of the Tree of Rome.              The

Tree of Rome knows its own leaves, knows its own shadows,
knows who to shelter                                                      knows

                    that brown is a color
                    capable of salvation,
                    because its own trunk
                              is brown.

Save the brown man of Asia who knows no other tree, for whom
the ungainly palm                                                                    is

                    the only tree.

Tell the brown man of Rome and of its cypress, poplar and oak,
the trees that still bow to the

greater majesty of the Tree of Rome. For there is no greater

                                                                          tree

than this, that has given up its own life for he who dwells
there, the presence who causes these shadows to fall, one upon
the other, in canonical succession,

                                                                          for

the Tree of Rome
is fed by shadows,                                                          the

shadows we leave behind. Whenever we fall under its shade, no
matter the color of our skin,

> Come, brown man, take off
> your black shadow, be cleansed.

Naked under the Tree of Rome,
bend your knees, bow
low to the roots.

> & suck. Be mothered.

The sap that flows from its roots is

> good sap, distilled from
> good seed

this sap
will mix with your blood, this sap
will grow into seed again,     this seed will grow

> Into a tree again.

> With its own shade
> to shadow your own
>           soul.

This is how we shall know each other, then, not by tattoos on
the outer skin                                        but

> by the trees that grow
> within us.        Thus:

> The Tree of Rome be with you.
> You will not wither. Climb.

So we all climb trees, and even if we don't know how,
we know what it takes,                    we know

how our own limbs must be used.          Branch on branch,
as it were, trunk on trunk,              so be it.

What a tree demands                 is likeness.

To climb a tree, one must be like a tree:        legs
rooted to ground, arms reahing out               as if

to hold up the sky.

    We must hold up God's sky,
    lest it fall too hard              on

our soft heads. We can bear only so much of him, only
so much, perhaps,
                                as the weight
                                of a cloud. And,

even then, not very much.                Now

then, are there now            two kinds

                              of trees?

Trees with heads only. And

trees with arms only.                    Now

        which one is the true tree?

Trees that have no arms                          say

        no prayers.

All prayers come from trees   with arms only. Arms
eternally spread, then heads lost in the forests of

                        their arms.

All trees with heads only are cursed trees. Their arms are mute.
They give no shade.

Some paltry instructions: plant
                              no coconut trees
                              in the churchyard

                              plant
                              no banana trees
                              in the churchyard

                              plant
                              no papaya trees
                              in the churchyard;

                                        bid the natives
                                        bring the produce
                                        from their own trees.

You will find the other native fruit trees
more cordial,                             more in keeping

        with this rooted theology
        of shade                          and arms. And you

will find them more restful in the afternoon where you may swing
hammocks                                                between

        mango trunks and atis trunks
        santol trunks and duhat trunks

                                        composing sermons
                                        in their shade
                                        adding up tithes
                                        in their shade
                                        eating sweetmeats
                                        in their shade
                                        burrping Latin

between long draughts of brewed beer, swinging the hammocks of
liver and spleen in the deeper shade of your bellies.

Remember well, friar sons of Augustine,
                    Dominic
                    and Francis,

this is why you must be cowled:               So that,

                              like favored trees,

your heads will stay bowed.                   So also,

                              like favored trees,

your hands will stay free,          free to reach up

without reaching               the sky.

     And with cowled gospel, give shade
to the innocent               Here, sit here,
                              brown man, and
                              listen, listen:

seek the shade always, seek the shade always, seek the shade always.

Harken, harken to the Tree of Rome.                    And

                         hang on to our sleeves as we reach up
                             to the sky.               Learn

                    to become good trees by these sleeves.

*The Fourth Fragment*
**Hammer and Nail**


The weight of his hammer
                    is
greater than the weight
                    of
seven bulls chained together.


                              What
are nails to his hammer but the subject
of all                         hammering?

                              For
hammering is an art, the object's how
to drive it straight through wood

                              without
having it bent like a penitent, with-
out splintering the wood, or having the
splinters
        splayed out like angel wings
because he has more than enough angels
in the ceiling of his house.

                              Suffer
the hammering on your crown for the
sake of his truth.            He, too,
has had his day with nails.

Hammer and nail. Each one completing
the other as prophesied:

                              The
hammer knows itself through the nail.

With the hammer the nail comes into being.

      The Roman way
is in becoming truly nail, avoiding rust
in the wood's embrace.

           Consider, then,
why nails have no arms. Are limbless, with-
out fingers, without toes.

There is only one hammer, you see.  The

hammer that falls on the limbless nail, for only
the limbless

            are helpless. Only the helpless
            need salvation in wood.  Are
            wed to the wood      by
            bonds stronger than arms.

Arms do not bind because arms tire of clutching.
An embrace in arms is finite,        he

who wields the hammer
     has no use

         for finite embraces.

            His

is the final embrace.

*Introibo ad domicilium Dei*
*Ad Deum que laetificat clavulum meum.*

I will go into God's dwelling place,
To God the joy of my nail.

        I am part of the roofbeams.

With my whole body pounded
into the woodwork,    my eyes

grow out of the crown of my head,                    Here
where the force of his hammer                         has
made me shine

                    I reflect the glory
                                        of candles lit

in the savage void.

                    Void!

All else beneath these roofbeams is a void, save where his arm
rests,
a disembodied arm, the hammer still clenched
in its fist.                    It rests

                    on top of a table,
            with the hammer's head upright

Proud, oh proud, in the soft, obsequious glow of candles lit

                                        in the savage void.

Savage, oh truly savage, is this void beneath the roofbeams.

                    Void!

                                        A pit
                                    without nails.

The savage echo

                    Hallooo, hammer
                                (hammer)
                                (hammer)
                                (hammer)

The savage void:

The arm without its body,

the hammer with no nails
                    to pound on.
No wood. No wood. The arms savaged
by this absence, the hammer savaged
                              by this lack,
                                this void

borne like a phantom traveler across a desert
(the arm, assuming legs, becomes a camel). But nails

do not bite into sand. Only wood can give us glory.

                                Stop.

The final bond, the wedding of wood and nail,

                                    here

let the splinters                   fall

                                    into

                                    the

                            void.

Here is the final embrace:              I displace

            wood

to become one with the     wood        I burrow

into wood to become one                with the

            wood                        I become

            wood                        I lose

    the meaning of nail                 I gain

the meaning of          wood                    I am held fast

and tight by            wood.

So Master Wood and Master Hammer

                        are joined

                        in battle against the void.

                        "Get thee behind us

                                    void!"

Enlist the nails

says Master Wood                    to Master Hammer:

            Make me strong.
            Give me nails.

            Pour them in
                        to my grain

            Pound them in
                        to my groin

I am everywhere

            groin, anyway,

I am everywhere

            grained, for I am            Master Wood

                                         made

                                         of all

                                         trees

                                                      in all

                                        the forests.

The nails will temper me, Master Hammer,

                                        and give me weight.

The nails will shine in the light of candles lit in the void.
Their crowns will be as a million eyes staring out into the void.

                        And I will be feared
in all my                                        manifestations

                        as roof
                        as roofbeam
                        as ceiling
                        as wall
                        as balustrade
                        as staircase
                        as post
                        as column
                        as door.

I will be feared                        for my nails
I will sow fear          in the void       with my nails

                        MY NAILS!

Remember that                        Master Hammer

                        MY NAILS!

Not yours                                        but mine
                Master Hammer

                        MY NAILS!

For it is           only me           Master Wood

who can make them truly

nails

For what are      nails                   if they are not

pounded                                          into

wood?

A nail
not pounded into wood is no nail. A nail becomes nail only when
pounded into wood.

I
am wood and in the depths of my being I carry the being of all nails

Become my nails
and I will make
you

NAILS

Be hammered      Be hammered            Be hammered

Raise

your heads

Raise

your heads

Be hammered

willingly

Be hammered            willingly

Enter into wood.

Become          truly nails              in my wood.

              Look up to the hammer

and say:                              "Come,

Master Hammer, come."                  "Take

me to       Master Wood."              "Make

me worthy       of his grain."          "Pound

me into       his groin."              "Wed

me to          wood."                  "Let

my crown shine from the woodwork, let my crown shine as an eye
into the void, let me stare out into the void that it may be conquered."

    But how, Master Wood,
does one conquer            the void?

    Can you, Master Hammer,
pound nail into            the void?

    From the void where I was no nail,
only something that could be a nail, a possible
                                        nail,
how was I known? How have I been, if not from
                                        nail,
then from something who could have been nail? A father
        who was only possible, a mother
        who was only possibly nail?

                                    Wood
                                    is
                                    fatherland.
                                    Wood is
                                    fatherland.

                                                Your
                                                father
                                                in wood
                                                is
                                                the father
                                                of
                                                all fathers.




*The Fifth Fragment*
**The Open Mouth**


Have you ever counted teeth, have you ever looked into
the                                             Open Mouth?

Do the teeth have ridges, do the canines speak up like
shafts, entering messages in flesh speared at its tips:

                              These are your bodies,
                                given up for me
                                              that I
                              may have eternal life.

                              This is your blood

                              splattered all across
                              my gums.

His molars are like chalices, and into their cavities fall
the blood of his victims.


                                                Does
the Open Mouth                                  close
to chew, or does it

have the victims chewed                                              first

by smaller mouths, yea, the mouths of priests, the open
mouths of priests whose mouths stay open, for each one

                                                            is

after Christus, after Oremus

within the limits of their physiognomy, within the limits of
the arteries of canon law, by leave of Rome where those dressed
in purple aspire to dentistry, by leave of other Roman clinics
                                                    where,
following Roman prescriptions, bishops are bidden

                                                    to

ordain smaller mouths, spread chrism on teeth.

See how the Mouth lies open, see how they open mouths in pulpit.

                                                    Burp.

                                            Swallow air.

                                            And chew.

Take your children to the fount that opens like a mouth.
Be good mothers and have candles line the rim

                                                    of

this fount that opens like a mouth. See how the candles
lined up along the rim of this fount

                                                    are

like teeth. Through this Holy Sacrament, we give
your children teeth.

Chew on catechetical food. Be good Indios, listen to the white
words that come from our pink mouths, follow your brown rajahs

this god we bring you                                                    the

god of the Open Mouth                                              that

your mouths too                                                    may

be open.

That you may speak white words without biting your tongues, that
you may say:

     Spain, yes, Spain, is the gateway to Rome.

And:

     Spain, yes, Spain, is the gateway to the
     white death that follows our brown death.

Receive, with open mouths, the god of the Open Mouth. Enter and
lie still while we prepare you for the passage. Lie still aswe bathe you
in oil. As we cut up your brains

     and
offer these for the glory of his kingdom. Be still.
Our teeth will cut you slowly, bit by bit. Your sacrifice will
be pleasing to his teeth.

         Accept them, Lord,
         brown as they are.
         Have mercy, O Lord,
         for they are brown.

Flesh is flesh and flesh will always be acceptable, this is the ruling
canon, beware only of blood paler than the red of his gums, this,
too, is a ruling canon.

              Chew
on these instructions: deliver
the savages

                  from their customs
                  preserve them

                  from cults
                  that command

                        animal
                        sacrifice.

Tell them that the Open Mouth eats nothing

                        but wind

                        and candlesmoke

                        and clouds

                        and souls.

Tell them to raise wind as they bite into

                        the Lord's Prayer.

Our father (gnash)
who art in heaven (gnash)
hallowed be thy name (gnash)
thy kingdom come (gnash)

                  thy will be done (exhale)


on earth (gnash)
as it is (gnash)
in heaven (gnash)
Give us this day (gnash)

                  our daily bread (exhale)

as we forgive those (gnash)
who trespass against us (gnash)
and lead us not (gnash)
into temptation (gnash)

          and forgive us our trespasses (exhale)

But deliver us (gnash)
from evil (gnash)

          and forgive us our trespasses (exhale)

And so with the Ave and the Gloria

          gnash and exhale

          raise wind like chaff.

All wind is pleasing to the Open Mouth
All wind is due        the Open Mouth

Prefigured by Jonas's whale
          exhale
          wail

            and like Jonas, sail
            into the pit.

Rise, smoke, and fill the Mouth with your curls and braids, and in
the Mouth form circles.                  He will

          eat these like chunks
          of clouds.        Oh,
          how he loves to eat
             clouds.

Remember        the        Friday      Prayer:

Abba, Father,
send me down
your clouds.

I thirst

and my mouth
lies open to

    your clouds.

Abba, Father,
O feed me

    glory

from
your clouds.

Let the smoke from your candles be white, be white as the smoke
that announces                              the Popes

in Rome, the news cradled in smoke because they know of no way
to make clouds                                   for

    his Open Mouth.
        Sad Rome. Sad Rome.

And if the eye of your candle's flame be round, we will call you

    Blessed. Blessed will you be among us
    who light candles to his Open Mouth.

    Blessed is blessed. Round is round.

    Search the eye of your candle's flame.
    Be among the chosen whose candleflames

    are not peaked like spears, are not
    pegged              like tears.

The Open Mouth                                    is open

                    round.

              As balls are round
              As eyes are    sometimes
                    round
              As circles are round
                    and
              As God's truth is round

              So is Rome's truth
                              bound.

The Open Mouth                                    is open
                    round.

              As an apeiron is round
              As the worlds growing out
                                        of it
                        are round
        As apples are              sometimes
                              round.

A mind as round as his mouth.
He has a mind as round as his mouth.

                              As round as an O.

Before his Open Mouth, begin all prayers

                        with an O.

O Maker
        O destroyer
                O Savior
                        O Redeemer
                                O Lord
                                O Master

110

                          O Shepherd
                            O Fish

While praying, bend forefinger to thumb
and with both hands shape Os

                    and raise them to the level
                    of your own mouth,

from where grow

                                          ladders.

The rungs round

                                as Os
              round
               as
               his
               mouth.

A prayered ladder                       going

              from
              round
                to
              Round.

Yea, a ladder from where no one

                        may be pulled

                                doune

make me round.


Round Lord

make me round

as my mouth.

As round as when

my thumb and forefinger              kiss each other.


Round Lord
make me round.

Round enough to fit

into your Open Mouth.

As

round as the rungs                              of my ladder

are round

and if these

be round

O make me have

round

soles.

Let my                                          toes

kiss the back                                   of

my soles.


Let me                                          climb

this ladder
with
rounded
soles.

Ascend! Ascend!
The Open Mouth bids you:                Ascend!
                                        Come!
                                        Climb!

Make yourself worthy, climb, make yourself truly worthy, climb,
make yourselftruly worthy of all that's in the OpenMouth, climb,
and climb as if all that is truly worthy is in this Open Mouth,
climb, for in this Open Mouth is all that is truly worthy, climb,
nothing that is worthy can be given to anyone who is not worthy,
climb into the Open Mouth, climb. Climb. Climb.

                        For here the world was
                        made

                            Mouth,

                        only Mouth, yes
                        only Mouth.

                        In the beginning
                        there was only

                            Mouth,

                        only Mouth, yes,
                        only Mouth.

                        And the world came out
                        of this

                            Mouth

                        this Mouth, yes,
                        this Mouth.

And when the Mouth thought it time to do so it opened,
yes, the Mouth opened

      and out of this came the world

      a round world that flew out
                of this

            Mouth.

A round world with round wings
        yes, round.

        For that was how
        it was,

        yes, round.

Round wings wrapped its round body,
a round message

      from the Mouth.


For Yea said the Mouth:                everything
                                everything

                                must begin round

                                everything
                                must be round

                                in the beginning:


The bellies of mothers must be round
The roots of trees must be round
The stems of plants and flowers
                                must be round

The stems that begin in any mother's belly

                                must be round

                               must begin
                               as something
                               that wraps it-
                               self round:

                               toes to the crown
                               of one's head

                               knees to the base
                               on one's chin

                               fingers down
                               to one's toes

                               all round
                               all round

For round is the shape of all beginnings

Just as round

is the shape of the Mouth that knows its end,

                        that knows when
                        the last round ball
                               of air

                        is coming
                        the last round ball
                               of air

That implodes within the lung

                      that fills it for the last time
                      that makes it round for
                               the last time
                      that inflates it for the

last time.

                              Like a balloon.

Round,
yes,
round.

Round,
yes,
round.

Round
is
the
mouth

             that opens for the last time
             that screams out the last balls
                                   of air

             That opens up to suck
             the father's          sky.

Round,
yes,
round.

The Open Mouth
is round.

# POETRY FROM NEW DAY


Alcantara, Adriana C. *Life of Jesus in Verse*
Allego, Antonio M. *Telling Triple*
Cuenca, Alfredo O. *Second Selected Poems* (O.P.)
Demetillo, Ricaredo. *Barter in Panay*
          *First and Last Fruits*
          *Lazarus Troubadour*
Dumdum, Simeon, Jr. *The Gift of Sleep* (O.P.)
          *Third World Opera*
Godinez-Ortega, Christine. *Lanterns in the Sun*
Goulet, Rosalina M. *Poems of Childhood*
Karmeli, Gabriel Ioseph. *Gethsemani*
Lanot, Marra PL. *Passion and Compassion*
Lolarga, Babeth. *The First Eye*
Magno, Rosa Maria. *Always There's a Thud*
WOMEN. *Filipina I*


---

Build up your own Filipiniana poetry collection by checking with your favorite bookstore in Metro Manila for the above titles, or contact NEW DAY Publishers (P.O. Box 167, 1100 Quezon City, or Tel. 99-80-46). Subscriptions to the *UPPER ROOM* (available in English, Cebuano, Tagalog, and Ilocano) also accepted.

In the United States, the official distributor for New Day books is: The CELLAR BOOK SHOP, 18090 Wyoming St., Detroit, Michigan 48221.